RALPH VAUGHAN WILLIAMS

ENGLISH FOLK SONG SUITE

DISTRIBUTED BY

7777 W. BLUEMOUND RD. P.O. BOX 13819 MILWAUKEE, WI 53213

Composer's Note

The tune My Bonny Boy is taken from *English County Songs* by kind permission of Miss L.E. Broadwood, J.A. Fuller-Maitland, Esq., and The Leadenhall Press. The tunes of Folk Songs from Somerset are introduced by kind permission of Cecil Sharp, Esq.

Notes regarding this revised edition

This edition (first printed in 2008) includes a newly engraved full score and set of parts. In addition to correcting engraving errors and omissions, the following changes have been made:

1. Measure rehearsal numbers added to the score and carried through to the parts
2. Titles of each of the folk songs added where they occur in the music
3. Horns notated in F on the score rather than E♭
4. Percussion split into two parts, and string bass separated from tuba

Instrumentation

1 – Full Score	4 – Solo & 1st B♭ Cornet
1 – Piccolo	4 – 2nd B♭ Cornet
8 – Flute	1 – B♭ Trumpet 1
2 – Oboe	1 – B♭ Trumpet 2
1 – E♭ Clarinet	2 – 1st & 2nd F Horn
3 – B♭ Solo Clarinet	2 – 3rd & 4th F Horn
3 – 1st B♭ Clarinet	2 – 1st Trombone
3 – 2nd B♭ Clarinet	2 – 2nd Trombone
3 – 3rd B♭ Clarinet	2 – Bass Trombone
1 – E♭ Alto Clarinet	2 – Euphonium B.C.
2 – B♭ Bass Clarinet	2 – Euphonium T.C.
1 – 1st Bassoon	4 – Tuba
1 – 2nd Bassoon	1 – String Bass
4 – E♭ Alto Saxophone	2 – Percussion 1
2 – B♭ Tenor Saxophone	Snare Drum, Bass Drum
2 – E♭ Baritone Saxophone	2 – Percussion 2
1 – B♭ Bass Saxophone	Cr. Cym., Triangle, Timpani
1 – B♭ Contra Bass Clarinet	

ENGLISH FOLK SONG SUITE

I. March – "Seventeen Come Sunday"

Ralph Vaughan Williams

48006174
979-0-051-66226-5

Engraved & Printed in Canada.

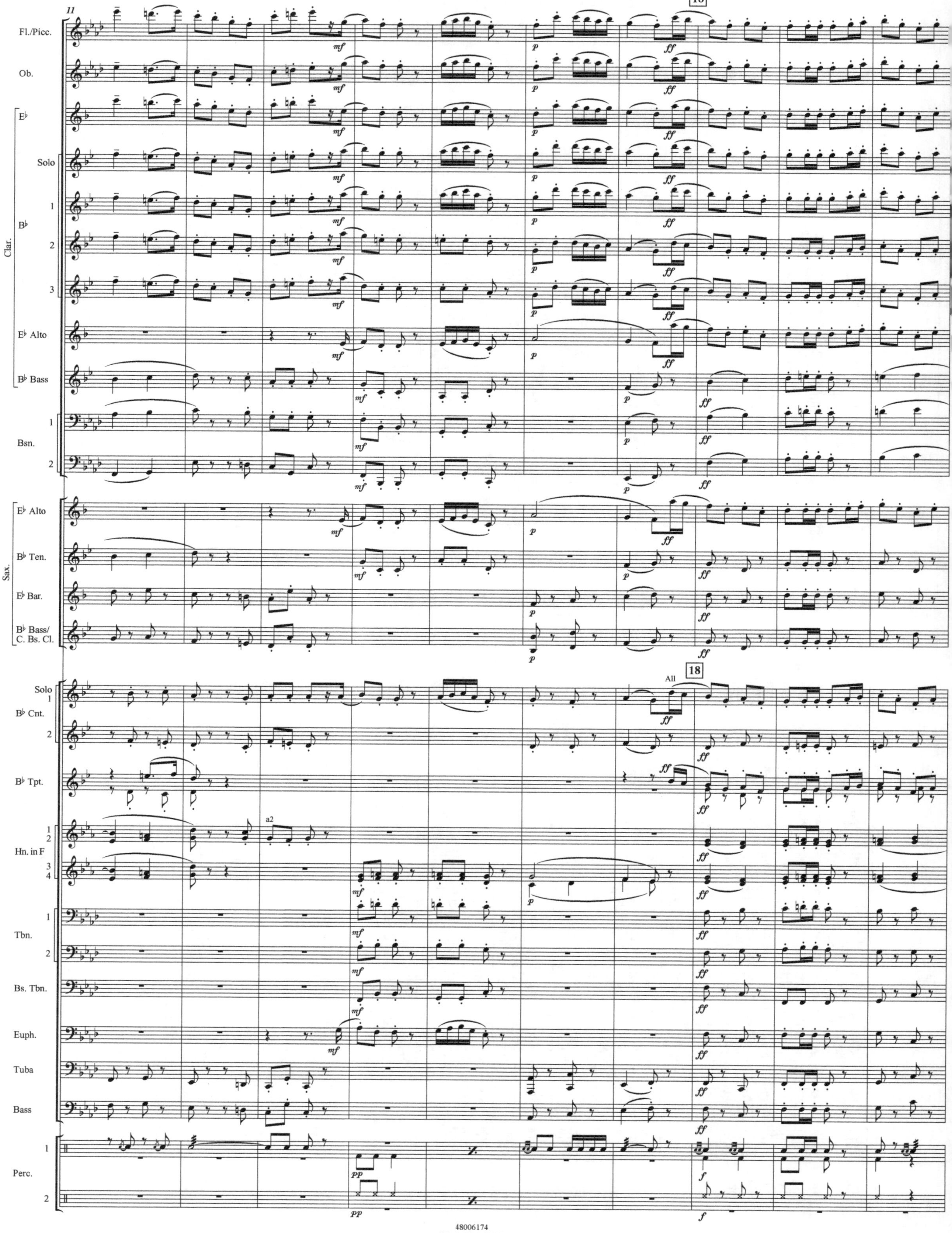

48006174
979-0-051-66226-5

6

54
+Picc. loco
Fl. 8va
Fl. only (loco)
+Picc.
a2
Fl./Picc.
Ob.
E♭
Solo
1
B♭
2
3
Clar.
E♭ Alto
B♭ Bass
1
Bsn.
2
E♭ Alto
B♭ Ten.
Sax.
E♭ Bar.
B♭ Bass/
C. Bs. Cl.
C. Bs. Cl.
alla pizz.
(-Bass Sax.)
Solo
1
B♭ Cnt.
2
p cantabile
B♭ Tpt.
+2.
1
2
Hn. in F
3
4
sim.
Tbn.
Bs. Tbn.
Euph.
Tuba
Bass
pizz.
arco
Perc.
ff marc.

48006174
979-0-051-66226-5

91
1.
2.
98
Fl./Picc.
Ob.
E♭
Solo
1
B♭
2
Clar.
3
E♭ Alto
B♭ Bass
1
Bsn.
2
E♭ Alto
B♭ Ten.
Sax.
E♭ Bar.
B♭ Bass/
C. Bs. Cl.
C. Bs. Cl.
alla pizz.
(-Bass Sax.)
Solo
1
B♭ Cnt.
2
B♭ Tpt.
1
2
Hn. in F
3
4
1
Tbn.
2
Bs. Tbn.
Euph.
Tuba
Bass
pizz.
1
Perc.
2
sim.
p
pp

48006174
979-0-051-66226-5

111
114
Fl./Picc.
Ob.
Solo
All
cantabile
Clar.
E♭
Solo
B♭
1
2
3
E♭ Alto
B♭ Bass
Bsn.
Sax.
E♭ Alto
B♭ Ten.
E♭ Bar.
B♭ Bass/ C. Bs. Cl.
+B. Sax. a2
B♭ Cnt.
B♭ Tpt.
+2.
Hn. in F
+4.
sim.
Tbn.
Bs. Tbn.
Euph.
Tuba
Bass
arco
Perc.

21
23
Fl./Picc.
Ob.
Clar.
E♭
Solo
B♭
1
2
3
E♭ Alto
B♭ Bass
Bsn.
1
2
Sax.
E♭ Alto
B♭ Ten.
E♭ Bar.
B♭ Bass/
C. Bs. Cl.
Solo
1
B♭ Cnt.
2
All
B♭ Tpt.
Hn. in F
1
2
3
4
a2
Tbn.
1
2
Bs. Tbn.
Euph.
Tuba
Bass
Perc.
1
2
pp
p
mp cantabile

"Green Bushes"

43 Poco Allegro (Scherzando)

48006174
979-0-051-66226-5

32

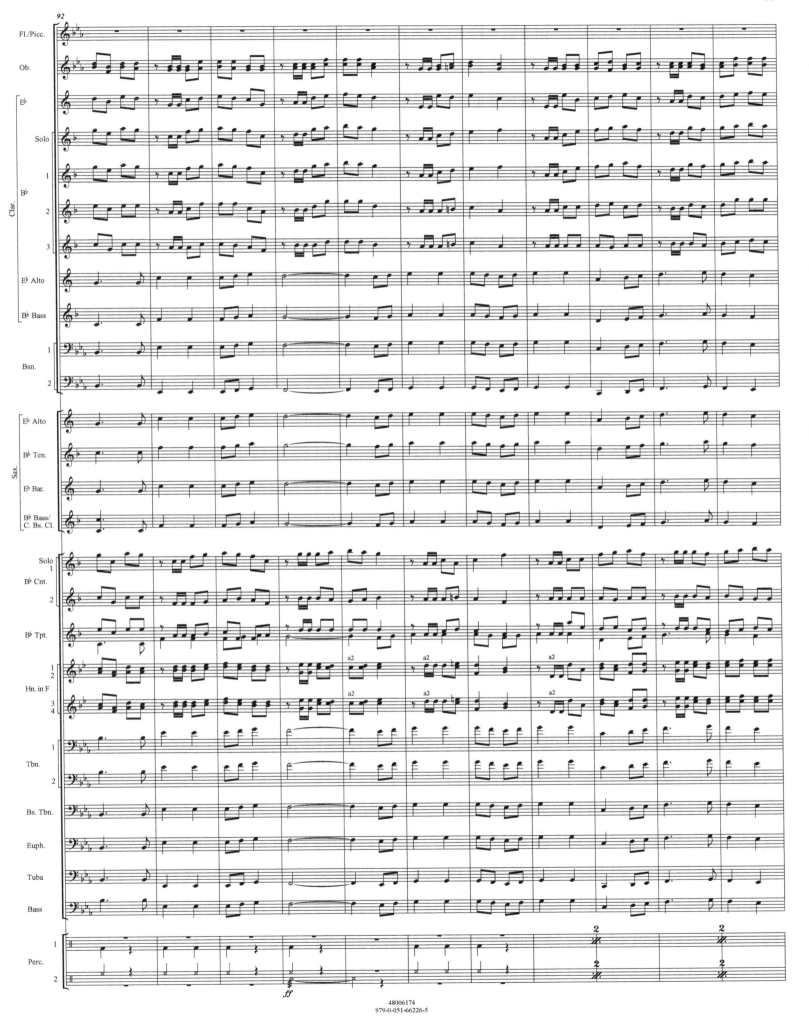

36